BOOKS BY ROBERT WATSON

Poems

Night Blooming Cactus   *1980*
Selected Poems   *1974*
Christmas In Las Vegas   *1971*
Advantages of Dark   *1966*
A Paper Horse   *1962*

Novels

Three Sides of the Mirror   *1966*
Lily Lang   *1977*

NIGHT BLOOMING CACTUS

NIGHT BLOOMING CACTUS

POEMS BY

ROBERT WATSON

ATHENEUM *NEW YORK*

1980

THESE POEMS HAVE BEEN PREVIOUSLY PUBLISHED AS FOLLOWS:
*God as Magician, Abandoned Husband, Repossessed,
    Lost:* POETRY
Distance: SHENANDOAH
*You Didn't Feel Much, Did You?, Please Write: Don't
    Phone:* GREENSBORO SUN
Life Across the Street: A GEOGRAPHY OF POETS (Bantam Books)
*Get Back Into The Closet All of You and Fast, A Childhood
    Friend Embezzles Five Million:* NANTUCKET REVIEW
Panthers at the Sherry Netherland Hotel: THE NEW YORKER
*Picture Taking, Roof Garden, Foreigners on 14th Street,
    Sidewalk in Summer:* THE ARTS JOURNAL
Victoria Woodhull: A CORADDI CHAPBOOK
A Simple Meal, Henry Flagler's Song: THE SOUTH CAROLINA REVIEW
A Good Life: THE GEORGIA REVIEW
Island of Bones: published as a chapbook by UNICORN PRESS. Passages of
    the poem have also appeared in SOUTHERN POETRY REVIEW and
    KEY WEST REVIEW OF THE ARTS

To *Betty Rean Watson*

CONTENTS

I

II

III

IV

I

PARADISE

always fades when we think of strawberries,
The first of a new spring or spring itself,
Entwined, we lovers, rinsed in warm white air:
Tulips strewing yellow and violet; lawn and trees
A green mist.

                        To think forever:
Lips sticky with strawberries, air sour milk
Our bodies attached like Siamese twins.
The stench of tulips, weather a monochrome.

Who could endure paradise a week?

You refuse a last strawberry, and I say,
I say, "Please God invent something new."
You say, "No, not God. *You* invent a new paradise."

I roll my mind out to a runway,
Adjust our seatbelts, the engines shriek.
You say, "I'm afraid." We lift, up, up.
You say, "All I can see is clouds."

Our paradise is clouds.   "Clouds?" Yes, clouds.

3

ABANDONED HUSBAND

Things in this life go wrong: zippers get stuck,
The car won't start, hearts break, whole cities slide
Under in earthquakes, planes bomb people dead,
Trains run late, checks bounce, mosquitoes bite
And the wind sighs, "Tough luck, tough luck."

This top, earth, whirs indifferent to you,
To me. The desert sizzles in the heart,
Ice cracks in the mind and tides gnaw our feet.
Today I watch a cold rain fall and ask:
"Why did you leave? I loved you. What went wrong?"

REPOSSESSED

Hot diggety! Here they come.
The sheriff blows his siren.
Eviction notice! The bank has foreclosed.
The Ford man drives off in our Ford.
Creditors come in trucks. There goes
The stove, the color TV next, deep freeze,
Stereo, sofa, chairs, tables, beds,
 (Boy, did we over-spend) power mower,
Vacuum. Mastercharge is wild:
They can't get back our trip to Spain.
These boys work fast, all's gone.

My wife and I dance on the lawn.
Whoopee. We are the lucky ones we are,
We can start again from scratch.
We are off to Nome or Key West,
With nothing but the clothes we wear.
Not a trace of our old life: new jobs,
New friends, nothing that's broken,
No clutter, a new sky

That will be bluer, air that will be colder
Or hotter than we have known before,
Barracuda or grizzly bears.
We will find a strangeness. She and I
Will embrace, new lovers in a fresh place.
We ascend the stairs arm in arm
To an empty attic where we will watch the dawn.

DISTANCE

In this country everything is so far apart:
Parents in Utah, children in Florida.
It's so vast it takes days by car to cross
Or bushels of money for a jet; and Alaska
Way up there and Hawaii way, way out there.
Take us at breakfast: You seem to be in L.A.,
I in New York, my coffee cup in Kansas.
My hand disappears from view. I can't see it
Any more than I can see you. Where are you
Across the table? Where are you?

I'VE PICKED GRIZZLY BEARS FOR NEIGHBORS NOT YOU

Alaska is so cold, so large, so far away
Unless you live there and then it's near.
Across the permafrost goes a grizzly bear.
He's looking for a cave to sleep all winter.
I wouldn't mind sleeping in a warm cave
In Alaska, dreaming of more Alaska that
Empty land with no one for miles around
At peace because nothing goes wrong
No power to short out, no car to stall,
All that empty space, far away space
So large, so white, so deep in dream with snow.

It's hard for me to get lost in this town
But I try. I seem to know all the streets
And paths. Yes, even where no streetlights are:
At night I can find my way, can name the lanes
Without signs, name the sleepers in their houses,
The dead who built them. How can I get lost?

I try to get lost, to take a wrong turn
That leads to a strange street, an unknown house
Where I ring the bell. The door creaks open
An inch. I say, "I am lost, very lost."
A voice answers in a tongue I do not know.
I rejoice. At last I am on the threshold
Of the unknown, unexplored. I am lost.

But then a car pulls up to the curbstone
And familiar voices call. "Hey there.
There he is. We found him." They found me.

She's out back with her telescope.
I don't know what she's looking for.
Only last year she learned to dive.
No, not sky but ocean, and yet
A week ago she flew straight up,
Helicoptering with a man
Who owns one, flew into a foam
Of clouds, sat in the plastic nose
Like in a giant soap bubble. Both
Of them looked, she said. "Looked?" I asked.
"Just looked."
     She dives to see the life
Below us, to name fish as now
She learns to name the stars. Today
She wants a photo of us naked.
"There are limits," I warned. She didn't
Hear me, went off into the yard.

Not there? You might try Timbuktu.

Nothing is like that first encounter,
When after months of mute half smiles
On street corners or at traffic signals,
That first chance encounter each strolling
Aimless in the starlight first separate
And then together, all thunder, lightning,
Hail and rain, a tornado of mind
And flesh until the storm blows out,
And then we meet by plan and walk
In steady slow rain of affection.
Now in the dust of habit
We sit in armchairs.
The wallpaper shows us a landscape:
Boys tending goats, asleep under trees
On a hill yellow with sunlight and age.

YOU DIDN'T FEEL MUCH, DID YOU?

It must be simple for some
To peel off clothes, do it
Without a thought, go home

To spouse, late news on TV
Without a backward thought
Of pregnancy or VD.

Sure as shooting I'd be stung
Not with remorse,
Or shame or fear

But by loss of the special
Like fireworks every night
Hot Cross buns as daily fare.

GET BACK INTO THE CLOSET ALL OF YOU
AND FAST

Nowadays even Bryn Mawr grads say "fuck"
At tennis games. At home no doubt their kids
Are doing recreational sex and pot.

No hang ups now! At shopping malls we see
Bare breasts on movie screens and gay guys preen
In bars we thought were ours. It's a damn shame.

In my day a hand job in a vacant lot
Was all we ever got, along with guilt.
I'm still repressed. "Let it all hang out,"

Is what they say. But I keep zippered up.
I wonder why? It's the old words I miss.
The inner turbulence that comes from "kiss"

Or "hug" or "breast," words like "ears," "knees," "thighs."
What can be more exciting than the eyes
Of one who says she loves you, though she lies.

PICTURE TAKING

They are making a movie in the park.
What a mess of actors, cameras, lights.
There are people making home movies
Of the making of the movie in the park.
There are people taking shots of each other
Taking shots of each other.
More people have cameras than don't.
It will take a normal adult a month
To look at all the printed pictures
Of this afternoon in the park, this stack
Of memories of men, women, children,
Of this one warm July afternoon
In this particular park.
What happens this afternoon in the park
Has no importance this afternoon:
Neither the light breeze nor the smell
Of hot dogs carried by the light breeze.

ROOF GARDEN

The soil goes up ten floors by elevator,
Bees by their own wings. Yes, bees are up here.

From this roof we see other roofs, but none
With so many flowers, vines, small trees all
So thick we can hide in this garden hauled
Up so many flights, the cars and people
Below invisible to us, we invisible
To them. How do bees find this high up patch?

Minute by minute the jets, one by one,
Slide overhead. Taxis swim up the Avenues.
Underground, subway trains squawk. Our doorman
Is on guard. Up in the roof garden hidden,
We sit oblivious to all but these bees.

A SIMPLE MEAL

Only the string beans are grown here.
The whiskey we drink comes from Scotland
By ship to New York, then trucked down
To our town. Our glasses are Danish.

The water travels in pipes right
Into our house. We make the ice.
Our crackers from London, our cheese
From France. The lamb was born and butchered

Half the world away, and frozen.
We will eat one leg of this beast
From Australia. We roast the leg
With gas piped up from Mexico

Only the string beans are grown here.
Our potatoes were dug in Idaho.
The wine is Italian.
For dessert have a Georgia peach.

* * *

I see Michelangelo stroll
In vineyards with Florence below.
Robert Burns scribbles beside
A clear, cold brook in Scotland.

A milkmaid in France strokes a cow.
Mice nibble crumbs in London
A kangaroo hops, smudge pots burn
On a frosty night, buffalo

Stampede. I'd like a sombrero
To wear when I see Elsinore.
Look, look a rabbit is eating beans
Outside the window. They're all gone.

The logistics of a seven course dinner
Is too much for me: Dover sole in flight,
Shrimpers drowning off Brownsville,
Elk plunging through forests,
Conches cringing in their shells.

FOREIGNERS ON 14TH STREET

Merchants stack goods on the sidewalk
To make the sidewalk look like home,
Home with open markets, bazaars.

Large suitcases on wheels sell best:
With one, so easy then to return home
Where all words and gestures were clear
As they can ever be and where
The food is known and comfortable
On the stomach, where little boys
Steal mangoes ripe on trees.
But these foreigners will never return,
And if they do . . . well, memories of a land
Are not what the land is now.

Also popular (one flight up) is
The Reader of Cards and Advisor,
Mrs. Estela who "never fails
To reunite the separated,
To lift you out of sorrow and trouble.
No heart so sad or home so dreary
That she cannot bring sunshine into."

What more could a foreigner ask:
On this streetcorner, large suitcases
On wheels and Mrs. Estela one flight up.

SIDEWALK IN SUMMER

In summer apartments are too small, hot
So what you see on the sidewalks, my God,
In wheelchairs, passed out in doorways maybe
Drunk or dead. Who knows? Mongolian idiots,
Guys in girls clothes, people
With no arms, no legs, no eyes or ears just,
Just, pieces of people. Others so old
They move inch, by inch, by inch, oh so slow.
And guys looking for fights, whores way, way past
Retirement. Winter keeps these remnants of people
Inside and the sidewalk looks pretty good
Though it's too cold for just hanging around
And enjoying yourself much.

PLEASE WRITE: DON'T PHONE

While there is mail there is hope.
After we have hung up I can't recall
Your words, and your voice sounds strange
Whether from distance, a bad cold, deceit
I don't know. When you call I'm asleep
Or bathing or my mouth is full of toast.

I can't think of what to say.
"We have rain"? "We have snow"?

Let us write instead: surely our fingers spread out
With pen on paper touch more of the mind's flesh
Than the sound waves moving from throat to lips
To phone, through wire, to one ear.
I can touch the paper you touch.
I can see you undressed in your calligraphy.
I can read you over and over.
I can read you day after day.
I can wait at the mailbox with my hair combed,
In my best suit.
I hang up. What did you say?
What did I say? Your phone call is gone.
I hold the envelope you addressed in my hand.
I hold the skin that covers you.

They leap from the ledge thirty floors up.
Panthers on all sides so high above

The street you don't see them. Or if you do,
If you by chance look up, you are not sure

What you see: greyhounds? panthers? stone or bronze?
Ah, they are panthers, green bronze panthers.

Why are they placed almost out of sight?
Why forever jumping toward the sky?

And why after years of passing have I
Never seen them, never looked up that high?

Then I looked still higher, above the ledge,
Where I saw a tower. See! See! from the top

Of the tower are more panthers that leap,
Nine more panthers radiate like spokes.

I don't understand why they are there.
Most of what is, seems outside my vision

Or if I at last see what has been hidden
I seldom know what it is that I see.

I had a vision of bronze panthers;
All night they leap at the roof of my mind.

He yanks a whole Spring out of his top hat
Of night: warm air, leaves, violets, daffodils.
Or maybe wraps up the town in ice.

His wand moves and children tumble from wombs.
Or he makes things disappear, say grandfathers
And snow, entire cities under volcanoes . . .

He palmed the universe out of his sleeve
Like a grenade, exploding it "bang,"
A giant Fourth of July rocket. Behold,

Our earth, the heavens, the beautiful debris
Still soaring beyond telescopes, beyond. . . .
It beats me. You flew, a bouquet from his wand

To me as I flew. I love you, I say
Before he tucks us with his wand away.

II

HENRY FLAGLER'S SONG

I invented Florida when I was old.
We lived in New York City in the cold.

I was retired from oil, I had some wealth;
Mary, my first wife, was in poor health.

We rode in my private railroad car.
Ah, the warm south surely would be her cure.

That winter we steamed into Jacksonville
Where I drew up Florida like my will:

I said I would bequeath to future men
Of wealth and station a temperate garden

By the sea which they could reach by yacht or rail
Where they could toast the sun with ginger ale.

Now in my holy city of St. Augustine,
My hotel Ponce de Leon can be seen:

Its many courts and cool retreats with fountains,
Water spraying from the mouths of dolphins.

That my civilization would prevail,
That all Florida could be coasted by rail

I built my roadbeds, bridges down the entire state.
Now its length my hotels punctuate.

My conquest is a land of orange trees,
Palms, Bougainvillaea, and warm salt seas.

After God, as artist, I have created most and best:
St. Augustine, Palm Beach, Miami, Key West.

It did not matter much that Mary died,
In Florida I found a younger bride.

VICTORIA WOODHULL

I

(Cell 11. Ludlow Street Jail. New York City. 1872)

> Sick in body
> Sick in mind,
> Sick at heart,
> I write these lines
> To ask if,
> Because I am a woman,
> I am to have no justice.

Old Commodore Vanderbilt set us up.
He wished to talk to his dead son. My sister
Tennessee, I'd see her whack the old rip
On his back. "Wake up, old boy." We'd begin.
I'd call up spirits and Ten-Ten would rub
That rich goat where he'd get the most delight.
Once I conjured up Sophia, his wife:
He wouldn't speak to her. "Business comes first,"
He said. "Let me talk to Jim Fisk. We'll get
Some good market tips." I aimed at his head
And Ten aimed lower down. Zip, we were made:
The first lady stock brokers in the world.
Our sign reads:

> ALL GENTLEMEN
> WILL STATE THEIR BUSINESS
> AND RETIRE AT ONCE!

Yes, to the rear for magnums of champagne.

As little girls in Homer, Ohio . . .
My younger sister Tennie C. was wild.

27

She was Miss Tennessee "The Wonder Child."
And sold her "Magneto Life Elixir,"
Two dollars a bottle, a cancer cure,
Sure fire. In Chicago this wonderful child
Opened her "Magnetic Infirmary."
I told fortunes there. But careless Ten sold
Joy to men, and one man died of the cure.

Ten was like a battery, her right hand
was positive and her left hand negative.
She poured out an electric charge all over
Poor sick men. The spirits I raised hovered
Overhead; and he seventy-five arose
The first time in years. We cured Vanderbilt.
But cures and stocks and money are not enough
For me. I want everything, my name on
Every lip: I want to be President.

WOODHULL & CAFLIN'S
WEEKLY
PROGRESS! FREE THOUGHT! UNTRAMMELED LIVES!

Demosthenes in a vision came to me.
He is the author of my public policy.
We are for free love. On the lecture stage
I can pull crowds bigger than anyone.
It was I, not Susan B. Anthony,
I was nominated for the Presidency,
The candidate of the Equal Right Party.
We are for women's rights and communism.
We are for free love . . .

"Are you a free lover," shouts the crowd. I shout: Yes I
am a free lover—I have an inalienable, constitutional,
right to love whom I may, as long or as short a period as
I can, to change that love every day I please!

At fifteen I wed Doctor Canning Woodhull,
Twice my age. He was a dear man, so dear;

And dearly devoted to cocaine and drink,
That when we divorced and I took James Blood
We let Canning Woodhull live on with us,
In the same room. Such is the strength of love.
My Colonel Blood is wise: he says,
My naturalness is righteous. I love
Whom I love. I never made a dollar
From love like Tennessee. My joy is pure.
Take that boy in Boston. He was nineteen,
From M.I.T., a virgin when he called
On us at Parker House in Boston. Blood
Good Blood, took a stroll. "Ruin me," said Bennie Tucker
Like a girl. And ruin him I did. That's love.

The Beecher-Tilton Scandal Case
The Detailed Statement of the Whole Matter
By Mrs. Woodhull

REPORTER: You speak like some weird prophetess,
                  madam.
MRS. WOODHULL: I am a prophetess—I am an evangel, I am
                  a Savior if you would see it; but I too,
                  come not to bring peace, but a sword.
Now on election eve, Tennessee and I
Are jailed. The charges: our *Weekly* is obscene.
Our *Weekly* is a blackmail sheet. Nonsense,
Our paper is no more obscene than Pope's
Poems, Shakespeare's plays. We are jailed
For telling the truth. But most we are jailed
Because we are women, we are women
Who lead untrammeled lives, honest women.
I had a man who admired me and sang:

          Sweetheart, no! You cannot go!
          Let me sit and hold you so.
          Adam did the same to Eve!
          Aimer, Aimer, c'est a vivre.

Here, listen to these letters from this man:

29

MY DEAREST VICTORIA:

> Put this under your pillow, dream of me,
> And gather the spirits above your nest
> And so goodnight.

THEODORE TILTON

and then this:

MY DEAREST VICTORIA:

> I made haste, while yet able to sit up,
> For I am giddy with ******* this morning.

THEODORE

But what a sorry **** he was compared
To Henry Ward Beecher, the famous preacher,
Who dallies hidden with Ted's wife.
I am in jail because Henry Ward Beecher
Is afraid of me, afraid I will write
About his carnal love with Theodore's wife.
I speak, I stand for truth. On stage I said,

"Didn't I know Theodore Tilton. I stayed with him at his house days and nights. I know Henry Ward Beecher! I have stayed with him at his house days and nights, and Gentlemen when I say I stayed with them, I mean no myth."

But he, the famous Henry Ward, he set
That Y.M.C.A. boy Anthony Comstock
To lock us up. They will not face the public
With their acts. They know neither love nor truth.
They would make women whores, make the divine
Profane, hidden, dark nasty. But I know
My naturalness is righteous. What is
Natural must be open and public.
On the streets of New York, in Chicago,
Boston, California, all over America
Millions and millions now sing:

Yes! Victoria we've selected
For our chosen head.
With Fred Douglass on the ticket
Yes, we will raise the dead.

Then around them let us rally
Without fear or dread
And next March, we'll put the Grundys
In their little bed.

Now that I am cast in prison, the world
Against me, I pray, and our cell lights up
With spirit light, the power of heaven shines
On your future president. God save you.
Wake up, Tennessee, the papers at last:
Look, look how they have cheated us again:

Ulysses S. Grant, Republican:	3,597,123 Votes
Horace Greeley, Democrat, Ind. Rep.:	2,834,125 Votes
Charles O'Connor, Taproot Democrat:	29,489 Votes
James Black, Prohibitionist:	5,607 Votes
Victoria C. Woodhull, Equal Rights	0 Votes

II
(Old Manor House, Bredon's Norton, Worcestershire,
  1926)

My chauffeur drove too slowly, I fired him.
My new one zips me around the countryside
To keep me moving. I don't want to sleep.
All night I sit upright in a straight chair.
I showed up Henry James who slandered me
In his "Siege of London": I married
John Biddulph Martin in 1883.
Then the Prince of Wales sent me some partridge.

No. No. I don't shake hands: too intimate,
Unsanitary. The Martin bank
Is far older than the Bank of England.
Our London house at 17 Hyde Park Gate,
A Pompeian Villa, has a domed ceiling
Of blue and gold. We have busts of Aphrodite
And Hermes, large silver statues of Nike
And Fortuna. I've been misunderstood.

I have been called a free lover. Not I.
I said "the love of God is free to all."
And I have told "The Naked Truth," that is
The human body is the Church of God.
My father was not an Irish immigrant,
A medicine man, they said, not a doctor.
He was descended from King Robert the Third
Of Scotland, James the 1st of England.
They said my Mother was a German-Jew,
A peddler's daughter. She was a Hummel
Of royal German blood. Now jealous folks
Malign me still my rich and noble blood.

Even Tennie, the Lady Cook, could not
Escape these lies though mistress of Monserrat,
The palace our Lord Byron loved and praised:
    On sloping mounds, or in the vale beneath
    Are domes where whilome kings did make repair.
At Monserrat Berenson, the critic, knelt
Before Fra Lippo Lippi's "Adoration
Of the Magi," Holbein portraits, oils
By Raphael, Rembrandt, Rubens just to name
The "rs" in Tennessee's art collection.
It was at Castle Monserrat our niece,
Our grandniece Utica wed Sir Thomas.
He is the leader of our Royal Symphony.
His father, a disgrace, made his fortune

With laxatives. You know that vulgar song:

> Hark the Herald angels sing
> Beecham's Pills are just the thing.
> Peace on earth and mercy mild
> Two for man one for child.

My dear daughter Lulu is so pure she never wed.
My son Bryon, a witless invalid, now long dead.

What I preach is not free love. I am known
As the priestess of propriety, decorum.
"Stop that ticklin' ticklin' ticklin' Jock."
Sir Harry Lauder sang those words in court.
But I made my vicar here at Bredon's
Norton ban that vile "Tickling Jock."
Not free love. I'm misunderstood. I stand
For "Stiripiculture" where the best blood
Will propagate the race. It's modern science.
Our motto is *Pacem Hominibus*
Habe, Bellum Cum Vitiis. It means
We are at peace with men, at war with vice.
I am bequeathing this Manor House,
The Hermes Lodge and Old Tithe Barn,
A twelfth century store house, and the land
To our Anglo-American Society.

At night I sit in a chair
Days I ride in my car
Anywhere, oh anywhere

Spirits no longer hover
Around my head. Demosthenes
Is mute.

All my friends, my enemies

Are dead. I have had wealth,
I have had power,

I have had love and a name:
Victoria Caflin Woodhull Blood Martin.
What next, what next?

I always knew. I don't know now.
I have had more than any woman
Who ever lived.

I have lived to get what I want.
I won all but one,
The Presidency, the White House.

They saw to that: Tilton, Beecher, Comstock.
All dead, all lies, all dead.
And I? What next?

GERALD MURPHY WATCHES TENDER IS THE NIGHT

(Inspired by Calvin Tomkins' *Living Well Is the Best Revenge*)

A Friday matinee at R.K.O.
In Nyack. I am the only customer.
My life, Sara's life, Zelda's and Scott's flows
Not on the screen, but in my mind,
Here in the palace of the impoverished,
The tasteless. I watch this film about us
That is not about us, yet I forget
In the darkness that nobody is here
But I, an old man of seventy-four.

The Divers were a fictive pair. Sara
and I were not. Sara wrote Scott, "You don't
Know what people are like, not even Zelda."

Did my life end thirty years ago
After twelve years of play in Europe?
Our villa in Antibes, our schooner *Weatherbird*.
Our guests Picasso, Diaghilev, Ernest,
Archie, Cole, Monty, Leger, Man Ray, Cocteau . . .
We'd start with sherry on the beach at ten,
And swim. No one in the western world
Had more style than Sara and I, no one.
Our days, dinner parties, dances were perfect.
We were the masters of the Riviera,
Of Paris. Our art was giving parties.
We made each day different from the last.
Only the invented part of life has joy.

The twenties died, the thirties came like the fog,
Pea soup. The wheel of fortune pointed down:
Father died in '31, one million bucks

In debt. Our two sons died. We closed up France
Forever. My father willed me Mark Cross,
A bankrupt leather store. Its motto is
"Everything for the rider but the horse."
For over twenty years I sold luggage,
Billfolds, what have you. And we called it life.
I am alive at the Nyack R.K.O.
Sara is home; she would not come with me.

I am the only person from my past
Who is not famous, one of the few alive:
Poor Zelda burnt up in a madhouse fire,
Last year Ernest blew out his brains.

I don't know why I put aside my paints,
My canvas. I did ten large paintings.
Quite good ones. Who wants to be second-rate?
I excelled; I was great at flower and fruit,
People arrangements. Party was my art form.
My work endured a few hours, then gone.
We stopped the music, blew the candles out.
I played jazz records, old Negro songs,
Cowboy music no one in France had heard.
Who alive has more joyful memories than
Sara and I? No one on earth today
Can live as we did, can know the men
Who changed the world of sound and sight as none
Have before or since. Do I exaggerate?
Am I a name dropper without a name?

The only life worthwhile is one of pleasure,
In style, of course. In nineteen twenty-three
I wore French sailors' striped jersey shirts,
White duck pants, white work cap. By season's end
Every man at Antibes was dressed as I.

Pop-corn. I smell pop-corn, stale as Yale
Was when I was 'Skull and Bones.' Lights are on.
Skull and Bones. Skull and Bones are dull as death.
"Everything for the horse but the rider
Everything for the rider but the horse."

III

AMONG CHURCHES

Surely if at any spot in the city
A spirit in seriousness should descend,
It would be here on the corner of Greene
And Fisher, and should hover over my bed.

My neighbors are three churches, a synagogue,
A funeral home. Processions of dead
Flow past my window daily to our
Cemetery out of view four blocks west.

Serious possessors of expensive cars
Curb them under the Sunday morning bells.
While I feed on the seven course Sunday
Daily News, I know that prayers must rise:

Yes, thousands and thousands on all four sides.
Surely a diagram of intersecting
Holy forces from church to church would pin
The Holy Ghost above my uncombed head.

Yet wings swirling like a helicopter's,
A figure lowered, swaying on a rope,
These do not occur. And I never venture
Outdoors to look roofward. I know I'll see . . .

Nothing, squirrels or a real helicopter
Stuttering between steeples. The Spirit
Here is hidden as in shopping malls
Or golf links, or bars that open at One.

But the dailiness of dead hauled off
Regally in Cadillac hearses, and then
The thousands of cars parked on Sunday,
These make me think. Of what I am not sure.

What might quadrangulate on the corner
Of Greene and Fisher over my Sunday news,
Sky dive down on the roof over my head
Has not. Next week, who knows? I like it here:

A glint of rose glass, puffs of organ music.
I'd be more serious about all this
If I could. Anyway I like the neighborhood.
It's safe, quiet, and nothing happens here.

A CHILDHOOD FRIEND EMBEZZLES FIVE MILLION

I

I had not heard your name for twenty years;
The *Times* account is brief: You have three sons,
A wife; your Aunt Minnie put up the bail.
Where the stolen money went is not clear.
How come with all that loot you did not run?

II

Your teacher Grandfather taught Dad Greek.
Your Mother played the best bridge in town.
Both you and I were born to local chic.
Our closets held jodhpurs, tennis rackets,
Ice-skates, skis, golf balls and dinner jackets.

III

We boys all wore white gloves to dancing school.
Now miles, decades away from our birth place
I seldom hear about my childhood friends.
I'm told the town is full of Puerto Ricans,
Negroes, other poor. Fled the whole white race.

IV

I've had two speeding tickets; once I thought
I might divorce my wife and quit my job.
Instead I sit tight, mired in common goodness
That I know is not goodness. My mind says,
O World tempt me, drive me to rape and rob.

V

I have seen tornados toss houses in the air
And armies of locusts strip farmlands bare,
Have seen whole forests blazing in the west,
The turbulence of Northern Lights on winter nights.
I've lived as if inert virtue were best.

VI

Richard, with your hand caught in the till,
Five million is a monumental theft,
But next week some guy will double it to ten.
Crimes such as yours are soon forgotten.
You are small potatoes compared to Joseph Stalin.

VII

Peculation I'm afraid never made
A man immortal. And I would not trade
My slim pension for the month's attention
You receive. Had you escaped with all the dough
Your hometown pals, if any, would applaud you though.

VIII

Richard, you make me feel small. You did try.
I've always lived below my means. Though you
May die in jail, disgraced in every eye,
Cast off by wife and kids, you can rely
On me to envy your outrageous deed
All others unheard from or dead you are my last hometown
    tie.

LIFE ACROSS THE STREET

When I call to the dead to speak, the graves
At midnight are silent. In the moonlight
The tombs are white houses on dark green lawns,
A city of houses without windows
Or doors. Even the wind is speechless now.

The graveyard lies across the street from me,
My own house of red brick where my wife sleeps,
And I insomniac lean against the iron
Fence that keeps back the living from the dead.
What should I anticipate? They won't tell.

My parents, other relatives live there,
And friends. Day follows day, year follows year
Until I know more people on that side
Than this. The living city shrinks, the silent
Grows. I have never gone anywhere.

Never travelled on a slow boat to China,
Skied the alps or dove from a coral reef.
I have climbed the nearest hill and there
Climbed a tree I climbed in childhood to see
The world I would explore in years to come:

It is my stamp collection buried in a drawer,
The atlas on its shelf, a telescope
I never use. Too young for one war
Too old for the next, I have lived in peace,
Some would say monotony. Not me.

My first lover lies under that little stone.
She married a brother of my wife and grew
Churchy near the end. He married again.
How I'd like to see her when my time comes
But I suppose the dead don't see . . . or touch.

No matter how much I ponder I can't
Figure out what the dead do. They're like
A gas, I guess, escaped from dust. One part there
In the grave, the rest expanding out, out
To form the atmosphere we breathe. I give up.

It is hard for me to believe the dead
Don't exist under the white stones under
The green lawns behind the iron fence,
Asleep as my wife is asleep upstairs.
Whether I'm right or wrong doesn't matter:

It's the comfort of belief, not the truth
That counts for me. At midnight at this division
Between life and death, holding to the fence—
Sleepy now—two worlds merge: the moon has clouded
Over, a ground fog rises. Are the dead

Rising to enfold me? I cross the street
Enter my darkened house, ascend to bed.
I have travelled more than round the world,
Further than Mars to the white houses across
The street and back to my brick house, my sleeping wife.

A GOOD LIFE

Memories of a good life are not enough;
The fade out begins. I run to beat the dark,
I swim to light my eyes. I give up drink,
I diet on yogurt, squash seeds, herbal tea.

I take the lotus position, meditate.
Arising I fly straight at the new day
(What's done, was done) ; make the new day
Fresh as home baked bread, blueberries bog ripe,
Clams dug, steamed the same hour. My mind receptive
As a child's. Yes, I could wish for hail storms,
A city in flames, a hovering harem,
A visit from an angel. No, I train
For a different kind of tomorrow today.
I run to beat the dark, I swim to light my eyes,
To see the usual I have passed by.

I need a vision: Let me see an apple
That is tart, firm from a tree, an orchard
In Vermont, an orchard in winter snowfall,
The orchard blank as a white sheet of paper.
I walk in this snow. It squeaks in sub-zero.

I will not look over my shoulder, behind
At my footsteps, at the disrupted snow.
I am not ready yet to be the past in the past.

IV

ISLAND OF BONES

On this island
The island of bones
Dogs bark, fighting cocks crow
Cats cry and the winds blow
In from the sea

I awake on my patio
Under palm trees and mango
Odor of aloe on the wind
Iced lime water by my side
In the warm south Keats yearned for.
It is always summer in the Keys
I sleep much and float in the warm
Buoyant waters of my dream.

See come, come sea, she waver, buoy banger
Tart water, fish full, piss warm:
Yellow tail, snapper, angels, eel, squid.
Voices blow from the pier, twist in salt air
Out to sea, he come, she come, air in sail,
Sun shimmer, surf silver, bodies roast
In oil. The pelicans dive for fish.
"Gua gua, gua gua," the little boys yell. "Hey puta."
The hulls of shrimpers glide toward
The Marquesas, the Dry Tortugas to Cozumel.

She lies on her back in a pink bikini
She removes the top
He kneels rubbing Copper Tone
Into her thighs.
"What's your name?" she asks him.
She sings beyond the genius of the sea.

Down, down, down into the neverwhere
Shed of all the above
Through coral canyons, pink sea fans
I dive to a new world, swim for my cure
With barracuda, tarpon, shrimp, sea horses, rays . . .

In 1622 the Atocha sank
A hurricane cracked it on a coral reef
Its 20 bronze cannon were no defense
Against the pirates of air and sea.
In the Archivo de las Indias
Documents say the Atocha,
A sailing bank vault, held
903 silver ingots
255,000 silver coins
161 pieces of gold bullion
47 troy tons of treasure
50 feet below the sea
30 miles from the Island of Bones.

Finders keepers, losers weepers.
The fire chief's red car
Runs cocaine from bar to bar.

"I take my enemies' names, write them down
On paper, put it in freezing compartment.
One enemy threw guinea peppers on
My porch. All are powerless, all frozen now.
My husband was seeing another woman.
I take one of his crotch hairs and make knots
In it, then drop it in that vase up there.
He's impotent now, can't do it to her
Or me. Go. I can't tell you more."

Down, down, down,
I've fallen down the coast
From Maine to the very end
From ice-floes and snow drifts,
I've reached the Southern end of land.
America's end, my own end.
In northern winters, the ground frozen
The blood frozen month after month,
I dreamt of warm water and palms.

"Hiss, spaugh, squeak.
Honey an effen tire's flat.
Now the fish is in the fat.
Jeez I've got to take a leak.
Splat, hiss, splat, dribble.
Watch out for coconuts.
Where's all the other people?
O.K., O.K., let's jack it up.
Clump up, clump up, clump up
Clump up, clump up, clump up.
Hey come back! After all I paid
For her drinks and never got . . .
Sssssssssssssssssss wump.
Blue light, blue light, blue light!
Snap, crackle pop.
Club, cuffs, squat, search.
Hi ya cop."

A tour train circles the island town
The tourists buy straw hats and shells.

"Getting it up is no sweat
It's finding the right piece
To get it up for into down, Right?"

Down, down, down.

"Well ya see it was this way
Bill and I was in Howie's bar flat broke
And Bill says, "See the nigger in the booth
He's a pusher like he's got dough
So turn him on." Like I'm to ball him
While Bill grabs all his bread
But soon's he gets it in me
Bill gives him the old boom boom
I don't know why in the head.
One dead nigger.
Cops got us on the seven miles bridge
Yeh twenty bucks but I won't swallow it."

Down, down, down, in that swinging old town.

"For four years chicken farming was my life
Until I learned to dive. I don't know
Why a man with a wife, four children would
Decide to dive for treasure. You say money.
Yes, of course, but I'd say the adventure
Like climbing unclimbed mountain peaks. My name
Is Fisher. I live out my name. I live
Like an inverted astronaut. Down, down, down
To the bottom of the sea among wrecks.
I am an archaeologist of sorts.
If I believed in Atlantis I would
Find Atlantis. I knew the Atocha
Sank 350 years ago.
For 12 years I've swept the ocean floor,
My boats logged 120,000 miles,
I've spent 2,500,000 bucks.
When at night my boat the Northwind last year
Sank Dirk, my son, Angela, his wife drowned . . .
It was Dirk who found the nine bronze cannon
Raised two and died. Some gold we've found, the bulk
Still lies nearby under sand I'll blast away.
By October I'll be rich. Here is a gold chalice.
This is a boatswain's whistle."

My Night Blooming Cactus
Is twenty feet tall.
Its buds, fist big, appear in June.
The flowers open only at night
When the moon is full.
My pale yellow flowers shine
For one night, for only one night
Then close at dawn and die.

Down, down, down.
It's rapture time
Under the Frangipani tree.
Whee. Whee. We.
I'll go down on you
You go down on me.
Mangoes, fresh mangoes
Get your mangoes here.

In the deep of my mind all things swim
Can I in my own deep find a rapture
And return to the surface, to the rim
Of the world where you await my capture
With coffee and the daily newspaper?

Down, down, down.
It's rapture time on the Keys.
Now for the weather:
The temperature is eighty-five degrees,
Out of the south a ten mile wind,
Waves are two feet inside the reef,
Three beyond the reef.
Today will be clear and sunny,
Now it's rapture time at the Pro Dive Shop,
Best deal on diving lessons in the Keys.
So pop right out for this week's sale on wet suits.
Remember: Key West divers do it deeper.

I bicycle from one ocean to another,
From the Atlantic to the Gulf, ten minutes
Coast to Coast. At El Casique
I eat Arroz Con Pollo with black beans
And bread. Spanish crackles in the air.
I don't understand one word.
I didn't want to get up today:
I lay in bed counting the girls I've made,
On one hand.
The sea of my mind is cloudy, its bottom
Stirred up. Weeds float on the top.
To live on memory is to live on tea and jello,
Yet blind with hope and cups of coffee
I cycle from sea to sea.

KEY LIME PIE
Combine 4 egg yolks
⅓ cup lime juice
One can condensed milk
Pour into graham cracker crust
Add whipped cream
Serve chilled.

"It's a matter of energy and space.
Today I've had an energy loss.
I live in such a little space
I have no money, no job, all day
In welfare offices, the county shrink,
Enrolling my son in day camp . . . he steals.
It's space, the narrowing of space we live in, love on.
My Baptist mother ran away to Oregon

To cure drunks at missions. She died
Of cancer at forty-two, but I'd say
She died from lack of space. She was a prude.
I paid my way through college with my body.
It's hard for me to get through to men;
Even the nicest want me in their beds.
I don't mind dying. I'm suicidal.
It's only the body, body space when
Mind space is where God can come through
I know I look twenty-five, but I'm thirty-two."

I sit here wishing for wishes
In the Pier House bar
Where I can see the shrimp boats
At the cocktail hour
And where movie stars play in the pool.

"Get your mangoes here
Fresh watermelon, bananas
Roasted peanuts, conch salad,
Conch salad makes you horny
And when you're hot you're hot."

Every one clapped when the sun went down
And the clouds went up in flame.

Robert Watson was educated at Williams College and The Johns Hopkins University, and later taught at both institutions. He attended the University of Zurich as a Swiss-American exchange fellow, and is currently Professor of English at the University of North Carolina at Greensboro. In 1977 he received an award from the American Academy and Institute of Arts and Letters. He is the author of two novels. *Night Blooming Cactus* is Robert Watson's fifth book of poems.